Using Cutters on Cakes

Dedication

I would like to dedicate this
book to my best friend
Carolyn Madigan and my father
Joel Monger, both of whom
would have loved to have seen
this book published – and would
have had plenty to say about it!

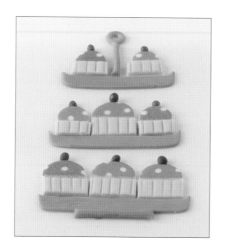

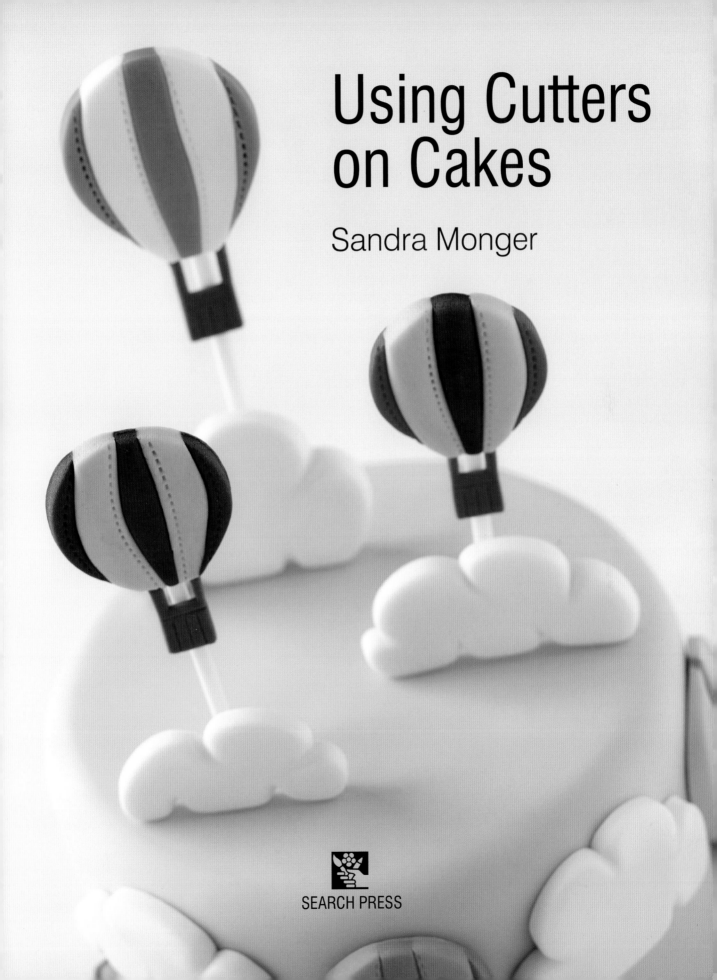

Using Cutters on Cakes

Sandra Monger

SEARCH PRESS

First published in Great Britain 2014

Search Press Limited
Wellwood, North Farm Road,
Tunbridge Wells, Kent TN2 3DR

Text copyright © Sandra Monger 2014

Photographs by Paul Bricknell at Search Press Studios
Author's portrait by Robin Pakes

Photographs and design copyright
© Search Press Ltd 2014

ISBN: 978-1-78221-033-7

Suppliers

If you have difficulty in obtaining any of the materials and equipment mentioned in this book, then please visit the Search Press website for details of suppliers:
www.searchpress.com

You are also invited to visit the author's website:
www.sandramongercakes.co.uk

Publisher's note

All the step-by-step photographs in this book feature the author, Sandra Monger, demonstrating how to decorate cakes using cutters. No models have been used.

Acknowledgements

Special thanks to Robin Pakes, my husband, for all his help and support; the team at Renshaw for supplying their wonderful range of icings; Stephen Benison for his support and advice; and to the team at Search Press for their help, support and patience.

Printed in China

CONTENTS

INTRODUCTION

I have always loved designing and decorating cakes but never believed that one day I would write a book about it. For me it is an unexpected twist in a creative journey, but more importantly it is an opportunity to share my ideas.

Cake decorating is fun and absorbing, while eating delicious cake is an almost perfect pleasure. But the ultimate enjoyment comes from giving someone special a cake you have designed, baked and decorated yourself. The aim of this book is to provide an introduction to creating fun and modern cake designs using cutters. It demonstrates how a basic range of cutters can be used to create many types of cake decoration, and ultimately it is about experimenting and developing your own skills and creativity.

Cutters give uniformity to designs and enable shapes to be repeated accurately and consistently. They can also provide quick yet striking results. At the same time, they can be used as tools to create other shapes and patterns. The possibilities are endless.

Thinking creatively about cutters means thinking about the different ways they can be used. It can mean rotating, stacking, cupping or embellishing shapes. It can also mean thinking about how they might be used with everyday household items, from pizza wheel cutters to scrubbing brushes and scouring pads.

The projects featured in this book are simply a demonstration of these ideas. Please feel free to copy and adapt them as you wish. Better still, use and develop the featured techniques to create your own designs and see where they take you on your own creative journey.

TOOLS AND MATERIALS

There is an exciting array of cake decorating materials and equipment. New tools, cutters and gadgets are coming onto the market all the time. For the new cake decorator, the choice can seem almost endless and even a little bewildering. A good starting point is to begin with a selection of basic cutter shapes and a rummage through the kitchen drawers to see what else can be used.

Cake baking

A cake should taste as good as it looks. The flavour is a matter of choice, but it is important that it is baked with care as it will form the base for the decoration that follows. A cake for decorating should have a firm yet light texture. Chocolate, madeira and fruit cakes are ideal.

Cake tins are available in all shapes and sizes. They should be greased and lined before use to ensure the cake can be turned out without damage to the crumb. Sponge cakes generally require only the base of the tin to be lined with the sides being greased. A fruit cake, because of the longer cooking time, requires the sides to be lined as well. Certain cake tins will require lining and greasing in a specific way. Always check your recipe and manufacturer's instructions.

A cake board can be used to present your decorated cake. It can also be covered, decorated and finished with a ribbon trim to complement the cake, forming part of the overall design. Two types of cake board are used in this book. A drum board is a thick board, generally used for display purposes, and a thinner, hard board which is used when stacking cakes.

A cake turntable or lazy susan is a very useful tool, which enables the cake to be rotated when being decorated. It also minimises the risk of unwanted marks and damage to the icing.

Cutters

Cutters are most commonly used to cut a given shape, such as a circle, square, heart or star. Some cutters have a built-in sprung plunger that both embosses a pattern and removes the cut shape.

Wheel and parallel-wheel cutters are used for cutting round templates and to form lengths of decorative coverings of consistent width. These cutters reduce distortion and stretching of paste when it is being cut.

Other items can be used as cutters. These include knives, pizza wheels, scissors, pinking shears and stationery punches. Try experimenting with different items and see what works.

Embellishers

Embellishers are used to add pattern, texture and expression to cut-out shapes and cake surfaces. Specialist sugarcraft embellishers include silicone veiners, embossing mats, moulds, stitching wheels and wheel embossers. Household items can also be used to create new and individual effects, for example scouring pads and brushes.

Cake coverings and edibles

Fondant (sugarpaste) icing

The main covering for both cakes and boards in this book is fondant (sugarpaste) icing. It can be bought ready to roll (although usually requires a little kneading) and in a range of colours. It can also be coloured with edible paste colour. Fondant can also be used as a modelling material if it is strengthened (see page 15) and can be textured and embellished.

Marzipan

Marzipan is a paste made of almonds and sugar. It can be used as a cake covering for a traditional fruit cake, where it forms a layer under the outer fondant (sugarpaste) covering. It can also be used as a modelling material and as a filling for sweets and cakes.

Modelling paste

Modelling paste is made by adding a strengthening agent to fondant (sugarpaste) to make it pliable and elastic. It dries a little stronger than fondant and is used where decorative items are required to hold their shape. It can be made at home or is available from sugarcraft suppliers.

Mexican paste (pastillage)

Mexican paste (also known as pastillage) is a form of sugar modelling paste that dries quickly and hard. It is used for the rigid and structural elements of a cake design that need to hold their shape, such as panels. It can be made at home or is available from sugarcraft suppliers.

Gum paste (flower paste)

Gum paste (also known as flower paste) is slower drying than Mexican paste and, as its name suggests, can be used for moulding and forming delicate shapes such as petals. It can be made at home or is available from sugarcraft suppliers.

Tip

Try making your own modelling paste, Mexican paste (pastillage) and gum paste (flower paste) – the recipes can be found on pages 14–15.

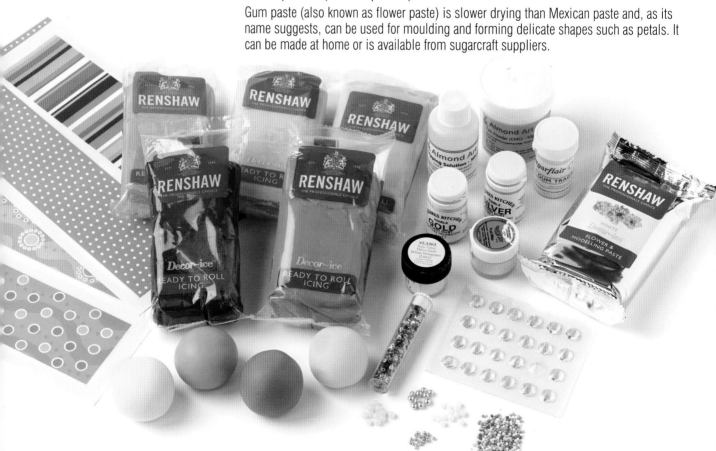

Royal icing

In this book, royal icing is used to fix decorative items in position. It is also a cake covering in its own right and is used for piping borders, patterns and decorations. It also forms the main ingredient of the gum paste recipe shown on page 14.

Jam (jelly)

Jam (also known as jelly) is used as a cake filling in traditional sponge cakes. Apricot jam is often used as a sticking agent when covering a fruit cake with marzipan, though any flavour, or even marmalade, can be used instead. Always boil the jam before using – this kills any mould spores that may be present.

Other edibles

Other edibles can be used for colouring, enhancing, patterning and embellishing. These can include paste and powder colours, confectionery glazes, lustres and glitters, sugar- and rice-paper transfer sheets, and edible sprinkles, gems and dragees.

Strengthening agents

CMC powder (also known as tylose) and gum tragacanth powder are used to give decorative pastes pliability, stretch and strength, making them suitable for flower making and modelling. CMC is a synthetic cellulose gum whilst gum tragacanth powder is a natural substance derived from the gum of several species of shrub. Both powders take 6 to 12 hours to work when added to a paste, so they are usually best left to rest overnight. They will need to be stored in an airtight plastic bag to prevent drying.

Dipping solution

Dipping solution is used in sugarcraft for creating glazes, and combining lustre and powder colours into a solution. It is also used for cleaning brushes after a glaze has been used. It is sometimes known as rejuvenator spirit or glaze cleaner. It contains isopropyl alcohol.

Guide to quantities needed

The following table shows the amount of fondant (sugarpaste) or royal icing needed to cover cakes of various shapes and sizes. Note that, for fondant, you will need additional fondant to cover the board (see page 19). When covering a cake with royal icing, you can add 1 teaspoon of glycerine to 450g (1lb) of royal icing to make it easier to cut, and the icing will not set as hard.

Size of cake	6in 15cm round	6in 15cm square	7in 18cm round	7in 18cm square	8in 20.5cm round	8in 20.5cm square	9in 23cm round	9in 23cm square	10in 25.5cm round	10in 25.5cm square	12in 30.5cm round	12in 30.5cm square
Quantity of fondant (sugarpaste) or marzipan to cover cake												
g/kg	750g	850g	800g	900g	1kg	1.25kg	1.25kg	1.5kg	1.5kg	1.8kg	2.1kg	2.35kg
ounces	1lb 10oz	1lb 14oz	1lb 12oz	2lb	2lb 4oz	2lb 12oz	2lb 12oz	31b 8oz	3lb 8oz	4lb	4lb 10oz	5lb 3oz
Quantity of royal icing required to cover cake												
g/kg	800g	1kg	900g	1kg	1kg	1.25kg	1.25kg	1.5kg	1.5kg	1.75kg	2kg	2.25kg
ounces	1lb 12oz	2lb 4oz	2lb	2lb 4oz	2lb 4oz	2lb 12oz	2lb 12oz	3lb 8oz	3lb 8oz	3lb 14oz	4lb 8oz	5lb

Other tools and materials

In addition to the tools and materials mentioned in the previous sections, other items are available that you will find very useful for cake decorating. Many of these you will probably already own, but none are particularly expensive to buy and are readily available from on-line retailers and specialist stores.

A large **rolling pin** is used for rolling out fondant (sugarpaste) and marzipan.

A selection of **rulers and a set square** are used for making templates and positioning decorations accurately. They can also be used as spacers when rolling pastes.

A **pastry brush** is used for applying apricot jam (jelly) to a cake side prior to coating with marzipan, or to lightly apply water to a crumb-coated cake before icing with fondant (sugarpaste).

A **piping bag and piping nozzle** you can make a piping bag very easily by simply cutting a triangular piece of baking parchment and coiling it into a cone shape (see page 13).

A **cornstarch (cornflour) dusting bag** (see page 13).

Smoothers and a **smedger** are used for smoothing and polishing icing and marzipan.

A **spirit level** is used to ensure that the sides of a cake are vertical and the top is flat.

A small, cranked **palette knife** is used to apply cake fillings and for picking up small and delicate sugar decorations.

A **scribing tool** is used to mark round a template to indicate the position of a decoration.

Edible felt-tip pens are used for drawing patterns on icing or to mark cake dowels before cutting.

A **ball tool** is used to cup, frill and shape petals and for embossing.

Artists' paintbrushes in various sizes are used for painting fine detail, colour-dusting sugar flowers or applying water when fixing decorations.

Vegetable shortening (e.g. Trex) is used to lightly grease rolling boards and is an ingredient in both Mexican and gum pastes (flower paste).

Spacers are used to ensure marzipan or fondant (sugarpaste) are rolled to an even thickness.

Cake dowels are used to provide structure and support within a stacked cake and can be used to support decorative features.

Lollipop sticks can be used to support decorative features.

Cocktail sticks have many uses, from marking and embossing to adding paste colours to icing and pastes.

A set of **measuring spoons** is essential when making Mexican and gum paste (flower paste) to ensure the ingredients are measured out accurately.

A **non-stick rolling board** is used for rolling out pastes when making decorative items.

A **small non-stick rolling pin** is used for rolling out modelling, Mexican and gum (flower) pastes.

A **foam pad** is used for shaping, frilling and cupping petals.

Plastic bags are used to store pastes and prevent them drying out.

Paper towels can be used when applying colour dusts.

String is for measuring vertical and horizontal cake dimensions when rolling out fondant (sugarpaste) or marzipan coverings.

Masking tape is used for fixing templates.

A **sugar shaker** is used for dusting with icing sugar when rolling out fondant (sugarpaste) or marzipan.

Scouring pads and **scrubbing brushes** are used for creating textures on fondant (sugarpaste) and modelling pastes.

A **non-toxic glue stick** is used for securing ribbon trims to drum boards.

Making a cornstarch (cornflour) dusting bag

A cornstarch (cornflour) dusting bag is used to create a light and even dusting of cornstarch on the rolling board or work surface to prevent paste from sticking. They are quick and easy to make.

1 Cut two squares of muslin approximately 18cm (7in) square. Lay one piece of muslin on top of the other. Place a spoonful of cornstarch into the middle of the square.

2 Gather up the edges of the square.

3 Secure with a rubber band.

Making a piping bag

Piping bags can be bought ready-made. They come in fabric and plastic varieties and in various sizes. You can also make them yourself from greaseproof paper or baking parchment.

1 Cut a triangle of greaseproof paper or baking parchment.

2 Curl the top right corner towards the point at the bottom and hold it in place. Then curl the top left corner round so that the corner meets the base, forming a cone.

3 Secure the cone by folding over the bottom points several times.

RECIPES

All of the icings and pastes used in this book can be bought commercially, but they are easy, and cheaper, to make yourself.

Royal icing

Royal icing is used to fix decorative items in position and for piping decorative patterns. It is also a cake covering in its own right and forms the main ingredient for the gum paste (flower paste) recipe in this book. You can keep home-made royal icing in the refrigerator for up to two days, but it must be covered and will need re-beating before use.

Meri-white or pasteurised dried egg whites should be used rather than fresh egg to minimise the risk of salmonella. To make up dried egg white, follow the pack instructions, then leave the dried whites to stand in the water for about 30 minutes in the refrigerator before use, otherwise the mix will be lumpy. The mixture can be strained to remove any lumps before adding to the icing sugar.

1 First, sift the icing sugar into an electric mixer bowl. Ensure the bowl is clean and grease free before starting.

2 Pour in half the made-up Meri-white or dried egg white mixture and a couple of drops of lemon juice. Using a K beater, beat on the slowest speed until all the icing is incorporated, then add the rest of the egg white mixture. It is a good idea to cover the bowl with a tea towel before you start mixing, otherwise icing sugar will explode everywhere when you switch on the machine.

3 Continue on a slow/medium speed for about two minutes until full peak is reached and the icing looks smooth and glossy.

4 Once you have made the royal icing, transfer it to a clean bowl and cover it straight away with either a damp, clean dish cloth or plastic food wrap (e.g. Clingfilm). Royal icing skins over very quickly so it must be covered at all times.

You will need

454g (1lb) icing sugar

70ml (2.5fl oz) made-up Meri-white or pasteurised dried egg whites

2 drops lemon juice

Gum paste (flower paste)

Gum paste (also known as flower paste) is quick and easy to make. It is also a great way to use up any left-over royal icing you may have. Gum paste will keep in the refrigerator for four weeks and can be frozen for several months.

1 Place the royal icing, gum tragacanth and CMC powder in a bowl. Mix well, adding a little icing sugar if the mixture is too soft.

2 Turn the paste out onto your worksurface and knead it, incorporating the vegetable shortening as you do so. Form the paste into a ball. Smear the paste very lightly with vegetable shortening and store it in an airtight plastic bag in the refrigerator for 24 hours before use.

You will need

250g (8¾oz) royal icing

2 x 5ml teaspoons gum tragacanth

1 x 5 ml teaspoon CMC powder

1 x 5ml teaspoon vegetable shortening

Mexican paste (pastillage)

Follow these quick and easy steps to make your own Mexican paste (pastillage). Mexican paste dries very hard and is ideal for making decorations that need to retain their shape. Like gum paste, it can be made in advance and stored in the refrigerator for up to four weeks, and can be frozen for several months.

1 Mix together the icing sugar, Meri-white and gum tragacanth in a small bowl using a spatula.

2 Add the vegetable shortening and mix well.

3 Add the water and mix it in.

4 Form the mixture into a paste using your hands. It will gradually become more stretchy and pliable.

5 Remove the paste from the bowl and knead it into a small ball. Seal it in an airtight plastic bag and store it at room temperature for 24 hours before use.

You will need

225g (8oz) icing sugar

1 x 5ml teaspoon Meri-white or pasteurised dried egg whites

3 x 5ml teaspoons gum tragacanth

½ x 5ml teaspoon vegetable shortening

6 x 5ml teaspoons cold water

Modelling paste

Simply add 1 x 5ml teaspoon of CMC powder to 225g (8oz) of fondant (sugarpaste) and knead them together thoroughly. Store the paste in an airtight bag and leave overnight before use. Modelling paste will keep for several months in an airtight bag. It does not need to be refrigerated.

Sugar glue

Sugar glue is used where a strong bond is required. It can be made easily at home by mixing 1 x 5ml teaspoon of CMC powder with 2 x tablespoons of water, then leaving the mixture to stand overnight to form a thick glue-like gel. More water can be added to thin it down if required. Store the sugar glue in the refrigerator.

Tip

When kneading paste, rub a little vegetable shortening (e.g. Trex) into your hands to prevent it from sticking to them.

Colouring paste

Mexican paste (pastillage), gum paste (flower paste) and modelling paste can all be coloured using edible paste colour.

1 Knead the paste to warm and soften it, then pick up a tiny amount of colour on a cocktail stick and transfer it to the paste.

2 Knead the colour into the paste until you obtain an even colour. Remember: you can always add more colour, but you can't take it away, so add it in small increments.

3 To obtain a marbled effect, simply knead the paste until you obtain the required effect.

COVERING CAKES

The projects in this book have been designed to help develop your skills in relation to a range of cake decorating techniques, beginning with how to achieve a firm, even covering for obtaining the best results from your cake decorating.

Covering a cake with marzipan

Before adding a fondant (sugarpaste) covering to your cake, prepare the cake surface by covering it with marzipan to ensure best results. Start by placing your cake upside-down on a cake board that is the same size as your cake.

Tip

Most cakes dome on top when baked. Cut off the top of the domed cake and level with a serrated knife.

Tip

The quantities of marzipan needed to cover different-sized cakes are provided on page 11, and are the same as those for fondant (sugarpaste).

1 Roll the marzipan into a long sausage, about 2cm (¾in) in diameter and long enough to go round the upper surface of the cake.

2 Gently press the marzipan round the top surface of the cake and cut off the excess to make a smooth join.

3 Flatten the marzipan ring firmly using a palette knife.

4 Flip the cake over and place it back down on the cake board.

5 Use small pieces of marzipan to plug any holes in the cake. Smooth over the marzipan with the palette knife to create a flat, even surface.

6 Brush boiled apricot jam (jelly) onto the top and sides of the cake in a thin, even layer.

7 Knead the marzipan to make it more pliable. Dust your worksurface with icing sugar then roll out the marzipan to a thickness of about 6mm (¼in).

8 If necessary, use spacers to ensure you roll the marzipan to an even thickness. Rotate the marzipan regularly to avoid it sticking to the worksurface.

9 Pick up the marzipan on the rolling pin and lay it over the cake.

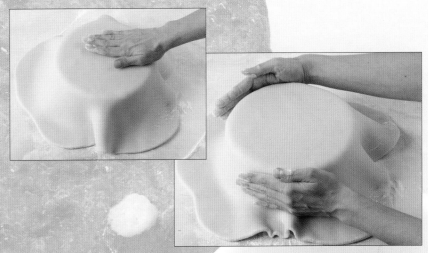

10 Smooth the top of the cake and ease out the folds on the sides of the cake with the palm of your hand using firm, circular movements.

11 Trim off the excess round the base of the cake using straight, vertical cuts with a sharp knife.

12 Use smoothers to smooth the sides of the cake with firm sideways movements. Smooth the top with circular movements.

13 Your cake is now ready for the fondant (sugarpaste) covering.

Covering a cake with fondant (sugarpaste)

Fondant can be applied over marzipan or over a buttercream or ganache crumb coat. Knead the fondant well before rolling to ensure that it is smooth and pliable. The quantities of fondant (sugarpaste) needed to cover different-sized cakes are provided on page 11.

1 Start by placing the marzipan-covered cake on a sheet of baking parchment, then place the cake and the baking parchment on a cake board that is larger than the cake.

2 Brush the surface of the marzipan with boiled water to create a clean surface for the fondant to adhere to.

3 Knead the fondant to warm it up and make it more pliable. Dust the worksurface with icing sugar and roll out the fondant to a thickness of 5–6mm (¼in). Use spacers if necessary.

Tip
Measure the distance across the top and down both sides of your cake to obtain the approximate width of fondant required.

4 Pick up the rolled fondant on the rolling pin and lay it over the cake.

5 Smooth over the top of the cake using a smoother to remove any air pockets and ensure an even finish.

6 Ease out the folds on the sides of the cake and smooth over the surface with your hands to ensure there are no air bubbles. Fold in the edges of the fondant at the base of the cake.

7 Trim off the excess round the base of the cake with a sharp knife using straight, vertical cuts.

8 Use smoothers to smooth the sides of the cake with firm sideways movements. Smooth the top of the cake with circular movements.

9 For a beautifully smooth finish, take a handful of fondant, make it into a flat ball and use it to polish the cake surface.

Covering a cake board with fondant (sugarpaste)

The cake board on which your decorated cake stands can be an integral part of the design. Cover it in a suitably coloured fondant (see page 15) in advance so that it has time to dry before you place the cake on it.

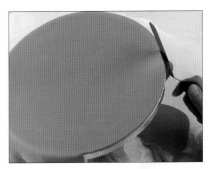

1 Knead the fondant, then sprinkle your worksurface with icing sugar and roll it out.

2 Lay the fondant over your board and smooth it with a smoother. Brush off any excess icing sugar.

3 Pick up the board and slice off the excess fondant with a palette knife.

4 Smooth the top of the board with a smoother, and smooth the edges with the palm of your hand.

Tip
If you are using brightly coloured fondant, do not knead it on a surface sprinkled with icing sugar. The sugar will mix into the fondant and be clearly visible.

Covering mini cakes and cupcakes

To cover mini cakes, follow the same method as for large cakes (see pages 16–19), but use a slightly thinner covering.

Cupcakes can be covered with a variety toppings such as ganache, buttercream, jam (jelly) and fondant (sugarpaste), and finished with decorative items formed from a range of materials. Why not add a delicious surprise in the form of a hidden filling?

1 If you wish to add a filling, scoop out a little hole and add some jam or buttercream (or both) before adding a covering to the cake.

2 Spread the filling thinly over the top of the cake too. This will provide something for the cake covering to stick on to.

3 Knead a little fondant (sugarpaste) to soften, then sprinkle some icing sugar on your worksurface and roll the fondant out thinly.

4 Choose a circle cutter that is slightly smaller than the top of your cake and cut out a circle.

5 Place the fondant circle on top of the cake.

6 Smooth the surface of the fondant covering gently with your fingers.

Tip

Any unused pieces of fondant can be rolled up and stored in a plastic bag for future use, providing it is clean and does not have cake crumbs or buttercream attached to it. It does not need to be stored in a refrigerator.

EMBELLISHING

Embellishing a decorative surface is an art in itself. From forming geometric patterns to creating naturalistic textures, embellishing goes hand-in-hand with using cutters.

Scrubbing brush

Press down firmly onto the paste (don't rub) to create the effect of grass, mud and ground. The same effect can be achieved with a scouring pad.

Embossing mat

This is reversible and can be used to create either a raised or a recessed pattern. Lay the mat on the paste, roll over it firmly and carefully lift it off.

Stitching wheel

Simply run the wheel carefully round the edge or over the surface of the paste to create a line that resembles stitching. Various designs are available.

Silicone veiner

Silicone veiners are soft and flexible tools used to create decorative impressions and reliefs on the surfaces of leaves and flowers. They are available in many varieties.

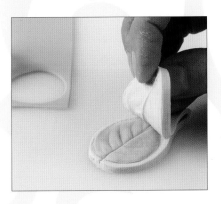

Varnishing

Confectionery glaze can be painted onto the paste with a paintbrush. Make sure the paintbrush is cleaned thoroughly in dipping solution after use.

Transfer sheet

Transfer sheets are printed, edible rice paper. Simply remove the backing, lightly moisten the paste, and apply the transfer. Smooth it into place with your fingers.

USING CUTTERS

To use cutters effectively, you need to know how to handle them correctly and how to achieve consistent results, such as rolling gum or Mexican pastes to an even thickness. Developing your cutter skills will enable you to use them in imaginative ways to create new shapes and forms, or as embellishers to give expression, pattern and texture to a decorative surface.

Rolling out the paste

Grease your rolling board with a tiny amount of vegetable shortening and roll out your paste between two metal rulers to achieve a very thin layer. Use a non-stick rolling pin.

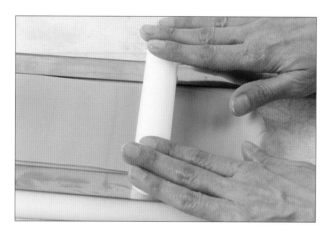

Using a knife

Use a sharp kitchen knife, and cut the paste using a see-saw motion. Avoid dragging the knife through the paste. The length of knife you choose should be one that allows you to make a single cut in one movement. A pizza wheel can also be used for cutting shapes – it's particularly useful for cutting round circles.

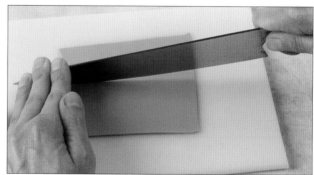

Using a wheel cutter

Run the wheel cutter firmly along a hard edge, for example a metal ruler. Make the cut in a single movement; avoid going over the same edge twice.

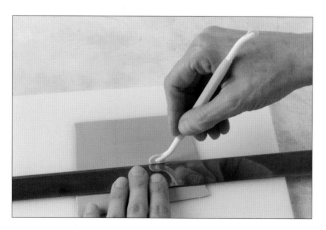

Using a piping nozzle

A piping nozzle is useful for cutting out tiny shapes. It can also be used as an embellisher. Simply press the nozzle into the paste and push out the shape with a cocktail stick.

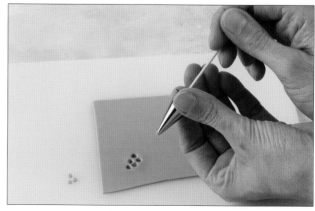

Using a plunger cutter

Plunger cutters are quick and easy to use. They cut the shape and release it. Some even emboss a pattern.

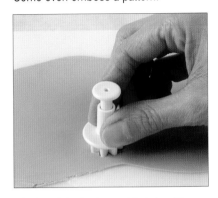

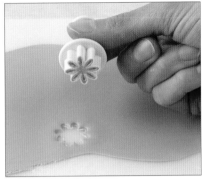

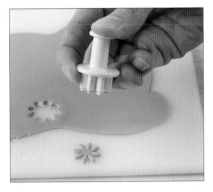

1 Sprinkle the board lightly with cornstarch (cornflour) then press the cutter firmly onto the paste. Press down on the cutter, not the plunger.

2 Lift the cutter cleanly away from the paste. The shape will be removed with it.

3 Press down on the plunger and the cut shape will drop out.

Using a metal cutter

Metal cutters are generally sharper than plungers, but the shapes are not quite as easy to remove. Roll out your paste as before, position the metal cutter (sharp edge down) and press down on it firmly. Lift the cutter away cleanly and press out the shape carefully with your fingers or an artists' paintbrush.

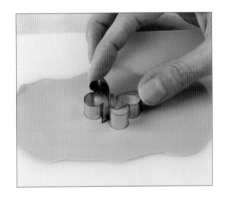

Tip
Always clean your cutter between uses using your fingers or a dry cloth to avoid mixing different colours.

Using a parallel wheel cutter

Also known as a ribbon cutter, this is available with a variety of different edges, and is used to cut even strips of paste. Hold the wheel cutter by the handles on either side and roll it firmly along the paste in a straight line. Carefully lift away the paste on either side of the strip.

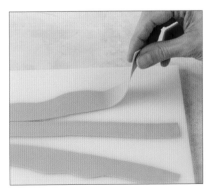

MOULDING AND SHAPING

The decorative elements made using cutters can be shaped and moulded into different forms. This can be done by hand or using a variety of items to cup, bend, fold and adapt them. Here are some simple shapes to get you started.

Making clouds

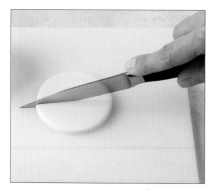

1 Roll out the modelling paste and cut out a circle using a metal circle cutter. Cut the circle in half cleanly with a sharp knife.

2 Use the corner of a square cutter to 'nip' out the points of the cloud.

3 Shape and smooth the points with your finger to make a cloud shape.

Wrapping strips round a shape

Cut the strips using a parallel wheel cutter (ribbon cutter). Curve the first strip round the shape, then continue outwards with the other strips. Work quickly to avoid the paste drying out. Trim the ends of the strips using a sharp knife.

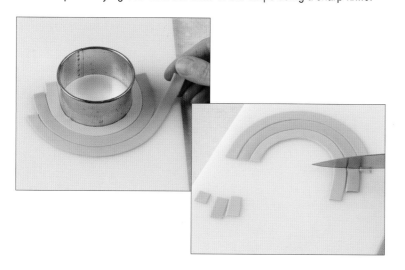

Making 3D shapes

Form a lump of paste into a ball of the required depth, and cut out the shape using a metal cutter. Push the paste out of the cutter using the end of a non-stick rolling pin.

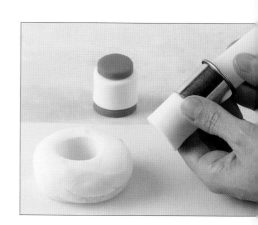

Shaping large flowers

1 To make simple, unfrilled, cupped flower shapes, rub a little vegetable shortening over the surface of the former (this can be any curved shape). Cut out a flower and lay it over the former. Gently press it down onto the surface and leave to dry overnight.

2 To add more movement to simple flower shapes, place the flower on a foam mat and rub the centre of each petal in a firm, circular motion using a ball tool. Rub the edges of the petals in the same way to give them a thin, wavy edge.

3 Flower shapes can also be layered. Separate the petals using small, torn pieces of tissue paper and allow to dry. This will give the flower depth.

Shaping small flowers

Use a plunger cutter to cut out the flower shapes and press them out onto a foam mat. Press down firmly into the foam mat as you do so. This will force the flower petals to curve upwards.

BABY SHOWER

This cute pastel design is suitable for any newborn baby celebration. Basic cut-out shapes are transformed and embossed to form the pretty pram design and the coordinating base-board decoration. Begin by placing the cake in the centre of the board. Edge the cake with white ribbon secured with a small dot of royal icing on the join. Edge the board with yellow ribbon secured with non-toxic glue.

You will need

15cm (6in) round fruit or sponge cake covered with pale yellow fondant (sugarpaste)

20.5cm (8in) round drum board covered with white fondant (sugarpaste)

Small amounts of pale blue, green, pink, yellow and grey modelling paste

Royal icing

Vegetable shortening

Pale yellow 15mm (⅝in) ribbon

White 15mm (⅝in) ribbon

Cornstarch (cornflour) dusting bag

Round cookie cutters, 85mm (3⅜in), 35mm (1½in), 30mm (1¼in) and 23mm (1in)

Circle cutter, 7mm (¼in)

Heart plunger cutter, 13mm (⅝in)

Smooth-blade kitchen knife

Artists' paintbrush

Small cranked palette knife

Non-toxic glue stick

1 Cut out several 23mm (1in) circles from the pink, blue and green paste. Cut them in half and place them round the base of the cake.

2 To make the pram, first cut a circle from the blue paste using the largest cookie cutter. Cut it in half with a knife and trim away a segment from each side using the edge of the 35mm (1½in) cutter.

3 Position the pram centrally on the top of the cake. Cut two grey outer wheels using the 35mm (1½in) cookie cutter and place these on the cake. Use a palette knife to avoid over-handling the shapes.

4 Cut two green circles using the 30mm (1¼in) cookie cutter and mark on the spokes using shallow cuts of the knife. Place these in the centre of the grey circles. Cut a green strip 86 x 5mm (3⅜ x ¼in) and position it along the top edge if the pram. For the hood, cut a pink circle using the 85mm (3⅜in) cutter and divide it into quarters. Mark radial spokes on one quarter using the knife and attach it to the cake.

Tip

To ensure the shapes stick securely, paint them with a light covering of water on the back just before positioning them on the cake.

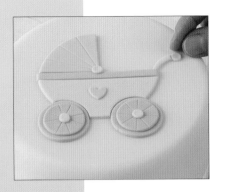

5 To finish, cut a little pink heart and three 7mm (¼in) yellow circles and position them on the cake. Use a curved off-cut for the handle, finished with a small circle of pink paste positioned on the end.

Tip

If you need to reposition a shape, don't try to remove it – simply slide it into its new position.

HEARTS AND FLOWERS

This romantic design is perfect for celebrating Valentine's Day and that most special of proposals. It introduces the use of a template and wheel cutter along with cutting and shaping using a plunger cutter. It also introduces modelling techniques using a small number of cutters. Begin by placing the cake in the centre of the board. Edge the cake with white ribbon secured with a small dot of royal icing on the join. Edge the board with red ribbon secured with non-toxic glue.

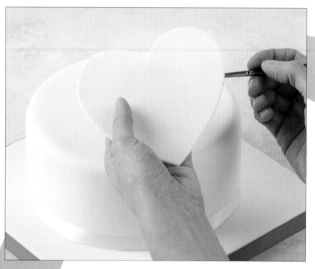

1 Roll out the pale pink paste and lay the heart template on top. Cut round it using the wheel cutter. Leave the heart to dry on a flat surface, then paint the back with water and position it on the top of the cake.

2 Make several small red and white flowers using the blossom plunger cutter. Cup the flowers as you press them out and attach an edible sugar pearl to the centre of each one using water.

You will need

- 18cm (7in) round fruit or sponge cake covered with white fondant (sugarpaste)
- 25.5cm (10in) square drum board covered with white fondant (sugarpaste)
- 4 cupcakes covered with pale pink fondant (sugarpaste)
- Red cupcake cases
- Small amounts of red, pale pink and white gum paste (flower paste)
- Small amount of light grey Mexican paste (pastillage)
- Royal icing
- Edible sugar pearls
- Edible sugar jelly gem
- Silver lustre powder
- Confectionery glaze
- Dipping solution
- Vegetable shortening
- Red 15mm (⅝in) ribbon
- White 15mm (⅝in) ribbon
- Cornstarch (cornflour) dusting bag
- Wheel or pizza cutter
- 13cm (5in) paper heart template (page 76)
- Circle cutters, 23mm (1in), 15mm (⅝in) and 11mm (½in)
- Heart plunger cutters, 13mm (⅝in) and 9mm (⅜in)
- Small blossom plunger cutter
- Heart cutter, 40mm (1½in)
- Piping bag and no. 1 piping nozzle
- Parallel wheel cutter or knife
- Smooth-blade kitchen knife
- Artists' paintbrush
- Small cranked palette knife
- Non-toxic glue stick

3 Position the red and white flowers alternately round the edge of the heart. Secure each one by putting a dab of water on the heart then positioning the flower on top.

4 Cut out seven red hearts using the 13mm (⅝in) cutter and attach one to the top of three of the cupcakes. Put the remaining four to one side.

5 To make the ring, cut out a circle from light grey Mexican paste using the 23mm (1in) circle cutter, then cut a smaller circle from the centre using the 15mm (⅝in) cutter. For the clasp, cut a tiny circle using the 11mm (½in) cutter and cup it using the end of the paintbrush.

6 Pipe a small dap of royal icing onto the ring and attach the clasp.

7 When dry, paint the ring with edible silver lustre powder mixed with confectionery glaze. Allow the silver to dry and insert an edible gem in the clasp (no need to add royal icing as the gem is already sticky). Ensure the paintbrush is thoroughly cleaned in dipping solution after use.

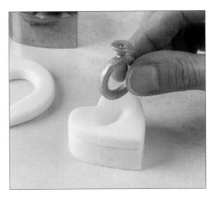

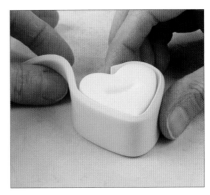

8 For the heart-shaped box, first cut two white hearts out of a thick piece of white paste using the 40mm (1½in) heart cutter. Glue them together with water.

9 Push the ring into the paste to create an indent in the top of the white heart.

10 Cut a strip of pale pink paste using the parallel wheel cutter or a knife. It needs to be as deep as the heart-shaped box and long enough to wrap round the outside. Moisten the side of the heart and stick the pink strip in place.

11 Hide the join in the pink strip with a red flower and insert the ring in the box. Place it on the fourth cupcake and position all four cupcakes on the square board. Cut eight tiny pink hearts using the 9mm (⅜in) heart plunger cutter and use these, and the four larger red hearts, to add a final decoration to the cake board.

TOY TRAIN

All aboard this magical toy train for an introduction to the techniques required to build up a simple sugar landscape and create texture using basic household items. This adorable children's birthday cake also develops the skills you need to use simple cut-out shapes as part of an overall design. Begin by texturing the covered board using the scrubbing brush (see page 21), then edge the board with the blue ribbon. Secure the ribbon with the non-toxic glue. Place the cake in the centre of the board.

1 Cut out the shapes for the sky and the ground from modelling paste using the wheel cutter and the template. Leave them to dry on a flat surface, then paint the backs with water and position the shapes on the top of the cake. Also cut a long strip of grey paste using the parallel wheel cutter or a sharp knife, paint the back with water and wrap this round the base of the cake. Trim off the ends.

You will need

25.5cm (10in) round fruit or sponge cake covered with green fondant (sugarpaste)

33cm (13in) round drum board covered with light grey fondant (sugarpaste)

Small amounts of modelling paste in pale blue, brown, grey and three shades of green

Paper template for landscape scene (page 77)

Small amounts of red, white, turquoise, purple, orange, yellow, pink and black gum paste (flower paste)

Vegetable shortening

Blue 15mm (⅝in) ribbon

Cornstarch (cornflour) dusting bag

Wheel or pizza cutter

Circle cutters, 23mm (1in), 15mm (⅝in), 11mm (½in) and 7mm (¼in)

Square cutters, 16mm (⅝in), 13mm (⅝in) and 8mm (¼in)

Square cookie cutters, 54mm (2¼in) and 35mm (1½in)

Small blossom plunger cutter

Parallel wheel cutter

No. 3 piping nozzle

Scrubbing brush to texture base-board icing

Parallel wheel cutter or knife

Smooth-blade kitchen knife

Artists' paintbrush

Small cranked palette knife

Non-toxic glue stick

Metal ruler

Cocktail stick

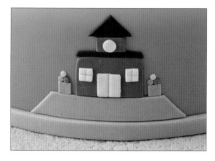

2 Cut a strip of grey paste approximately 85 x 15mm (3⅜ x ⅝in) and angle the sides with a knife to make the station platform. Also cut two small grey squares using the 8mm (¼in) square cutter and a small brown square using the 16mm (⅝in) square cutter. Cut a brown square using the 35mm (1½in) cutter and cut it in half to make a rectangle.

3 For the pointed station roof, cut a black square from gum paste using the 16mm (⅝in) cutter and cut it in half diagonally. For the flat roof, cut a narrow black strip and angle the sides with a knife. Cut the windows, doors and clock from white paste using 7mm (¼in) circle and the 8mm (¼in) and 13mm (⅝in) square cutters. Mark the panes and the centre of the door using the edge of the knife. For the flowers, use the piping nozzle to cut tiny circles from red, pink and yellow paste.

4 Arrange all the components of the station on the front of the cake, painting the backs with water to secure them.

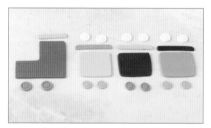

5 Cut out the components for the train. For the engine, cut a red square using the 54mm (2¼in) square cutter and remove a quarter using the same cutter. Mark on the lines using the edge of the knife. Cut out the white window using the 16mm (⅝in) square cutter, and use the same cutter to cut out the red triangular shapes for the front of the engine and the funnel.

6 Next cut three different coloured squares for the three carriages using the 35mm (1½in) square cutter, and cut four strips in different colours for the roofs. For the wheels, cut four blue and four green circles using the 15mm (⅝in) and 11mm (½in) cutters, and emboss them using the 7mm (¼in) cutter. Use the same cutter for the six white windows and emboss them in the same way.

7 Cut out three blue rectangles using the 13mm (⅝in) square cutter. Cut these in half to give rectangles for the couplings and mark on the rivets using the end of the piping nozzle. The puffs of steam are circles of white paste cut out using the 23mm (1in) and 15mm (⅝in) circle cutters, with little sections pushed in using a cocktail stick to create a scalloped edge.

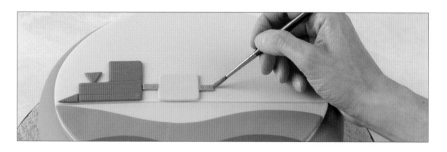

8 Attach all the train parts to the top of the cake, working left to right and sticking them in place with water painted on the backs of the shapes.

9 Once the train is in place, attach the remaining elements. Cut out some tiny coloured flowers using the small blossom plunger cutter and attach them to the grass.

10 For the tracks, cut a long brown strip approximately 25mm (1in) wide and cut off the individual sleepers using a sharp knife.

11 Secure the sleepers round the cake base. For the rails, cut two thin, grey strips using the parallel wheel cutter or a knife. Brush the sleepers with water where they will lie and place the tracks down carefully. Do this before the paste dries out so that they curve easily.

HOT-AIR BALLOONS

This uplifting design uses cutters and embellishers to create a summer landscape complete with clouds and balloons. Icing the decorations onto lollipop sticks lifts the decorative scene and gives height to the design. Begin by securing the ribbon round the cake base using the non-toxic glue and placing the cake in the centre of the board.

You will need

15cm (6in) round fruit or sponge cake, 13cm (5in) deep, covered with pale blue fondant (sugarpaste)

20.5cm (8in) round drum board covered with green fondant (sugarpaste)

Small amounts of dark and mid green, white, yellow, orange, red, fuchsia pink, purple and light brown modelling paste

Small amounts of mid brown gum paste

Vegetable shortening

Purple 15mm (⅝in) ribbon

Cornstarch (cornflour) dusting bag

Parallel wheel cutter

Wheel or pizza cutter

Round cookie cutters, 85mm (3⅜in), 65mm (2½in) and 50mm (2in)

Rectangular cutters, 25 x 14mm (1 x ⅝in) and 20 x 11mm (¾ x ½in)

Rose petal cutters, 63mm (2½in) and 54mm (2¼in) long

Small blossom plunger cutters, 13mm (⅝in) and 10mm (½in)

Stitching wheel

Piping bag and no. 2 piping nozzle

Lollipop sticks

Smooth-blade kitchen knife

Artists' paintbrush

Royal icing

Small cranked palette knife

Non-toxic glue stick

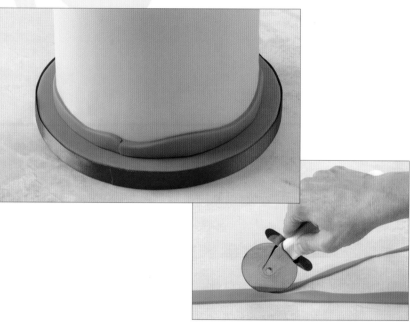

1 Cut a strip of mid green paste using the parallel wheel cutter, long enough to fit round the base of the cake. Create a wavy edge on one side using a wheel cutter or pizza cutter. Attach the strip to the base of the cake and trim off the excess. Apply water to the cake first so that the paste sticks.

2 Make four or five clouds in several sizes (see page 24). Also cut ten or more different-sized flower shapes from dark green paste using the blossom cutters, then cut ten more from the mid green paste and cut them in half for the shrubs. The tree trunks are brown rectangles cut with a knife.

36

3 For each balloon, make five small balls of paste and roll them into approximately 6cm (2¼in) lengths, tapered at each end.

4 Place them in the right order, then coat the inner sides with water and push them together. Squeeze the ends to make a balloon shape.

5 Use a rose petal cutter to cut out the balloon. Make six or seven all together, using two different sizes of rose petal cutter.

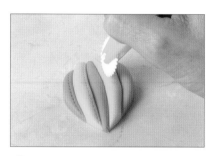

6 Use the stitching wheel to mark a stitch line along some of the stripes (there's no need to mark all of them).

7 Trim off the base of the balloon with a knife. For the basket, cut a mid brown rectangle of gum paste using the larger of the two rectangular cutters, then cut a smaller rectangle from one side using the smaller cutter.

8 Emboss the basket using a knife.

9 Attach the light elements to the side of the cake using water applied to the back of each shape with a paintbrush. Attach the heavier elements such as the clouds and balloons with royal icing either brushed or piped onto the back of the items for a secure fix. Retain three clouds and three balloons for decorating the top of the cake.

Tip
Remember that if you need to reposition a shape, don't try to remove it – simply slide it into its new position.

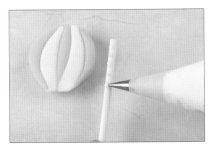

10 For each of the balloons on the top of the cake, pipe small dots of royal icing along the top of a lollipop stick.

11 Press the lollipop stick firmly to the back of the balloon, making sure it is straight. Allow to dry for several hours for a firm bond.

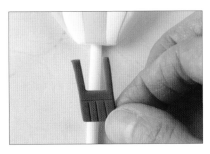

12 Pipe a tiny dot of icing on the back of the basket and attach it just below the balloon.

13 Pipe dots of royal icing along the base of each cloud and press the clouds firmly in place on top of the cake so that they all face the same way. Push the balloons into the top of the cake, behind the clouds.

39

SPRINGTIME

Just a few rotations of a cutter and some embossing techniques were used to create the cheeky bunny on top of this cheerful springtime cake. Begin by placing the cake in the centre of the board and edging the board with yellow ribbon. Secure the ribbon with the non-toxic glue.

1 For the grass, cut various circles of mid green paste using the 35mm (1½in) and 50mm (2in) cutters and cut them in half with a knife. Nip out tiny sections from the curved edge using the tip of the heart plunger cutter. Attach them to the base of the cake using water, retaining two for the top of the cake.

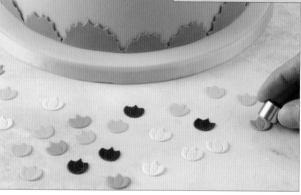

2 To make the tulips, cut out circles of coloured paste using the 15mm (⅝in) and 11mm (½in) cutters, then remove two tiny sections from the top of each one using the tip of the heart plunger cutter. Emboss each flower using the edge of the same circle cutter to create petals. Make several tulips in various colours.

3 For the stems round the edge of the cake, roll a very thin sausage of dark green paste and cut it into 2cm (¾in) sections. Make six further stems using mid green paste and put them to one side, along with six tulips. These will be used to decorate the top. To attach each stem to the side of the cake, lay a single brushstroke of water onto the cake and push on the stem. Brush on a little water above the stem and attach a flower. Manipulate them into place using the paintbrush. Curve the flowers in different directions.

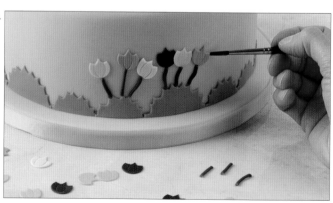

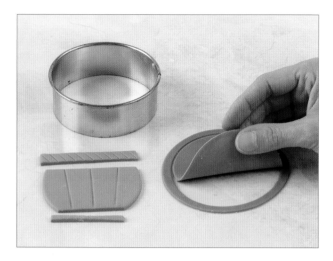

4 For the basket, cut out a circle using the 80mm (3⅛in) round cookie cutter and trim off the top and the bottom with a knife. Cut off the curved edges of the two trimmed-off pieces to make two narrow strips for the top and bottom edges of the basket. Emboss these and the basket with a knife. For the handle, cut a large circle using the 85mm (3⅜in) round cookie cutter, then cut out and remove a slightly smaller circle from the middle.

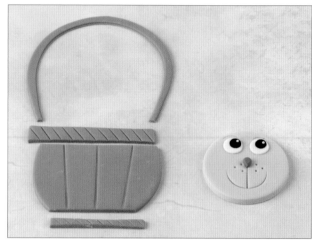

5 Cut a small segment out of the brown circle and open it out to form the handle. To make the rabbit's face, cut out a grey circle using the 50mm (2in) cookie cutter. Emboss the smile with the 25mm (1in) circle cutter and mark the muzzle and whiskers with a knife and cocktail stick. Cut two white circles using the 11mm (½in) cutter and two black and two pink circles using the 7mm (¼in) cutter. Form a tiny ball of brown into a teardrop-shaped nose and fix in position with a little water. The glints in the eyes are made with tiny specks of white.

6 Make the neck by cutting a small grey rectangle, then angling the edges. For the paws, use the 15mm (⅝in) circle cutter and emboss the shapes using the knife. For the ears, cut a circle using the 65mm (2½in) cookie cutter and use a smaller circle cutter to cut out a crescent-shaped segment.

Tip

Lay out the shapes in their correct positions on your worksurface as you make them. This will ensure they all fit together properly and you are happy with the arrangement before attaching them to your cake.

7 Cut the segment in half using the edge of the same cutter.

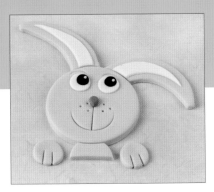

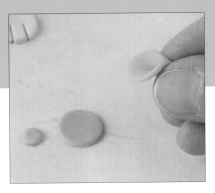

8 Round off the ends of the ears and position them on the rabbit's head. Make the white, inner parts of the ears in the same way, but using smaller cutters. Without trimming off the ends, attach the inner pieces to the ears using water.

9 For the bow, cut two small orange circles using the 15mm (⅝in) cutter, and a single, smaller circle for the knot. Pinch the end of each larger circle to form the bow shape.

10 Paint water onto the backs of the basket components and attach them centrally to the top of the cake.

11 Attach the rabbit and the bow in the same way, followed by the remaining pieces of grass and tulips.

WINTER ROBIN

This chirpy Christmas favourite will bring cheer to any Yuletide table. The design uses a side template to shape a decorative swagged border, a candy-cane rope twist and needlecraft-inspired appliqué robin for festive effect. Begin by edging the board with green ribbon. Secure the ribbon with non-toxic glue. Position the cake in the centre of the board.

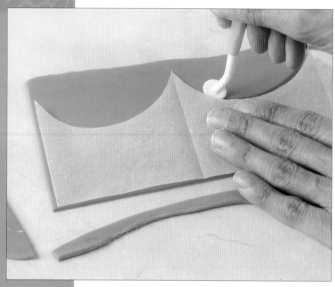

1 Cut an 8cm (3¼in) deep strip of baking parchment, long enough to fit once round the cake. Fold it into eight sections, draw a curve on the top edge and cut along the curve. Unfold to reveal the template. Roll out a strip of mid green paste approximately 12cm (4¾in) wide. Lay the template on top and trim off the base and sides with a knife. Cut round the curves using the wheel cutter.

2 Cut out several dark green holly leaves using the holly leaf plunger cutter.

Tip
Give the leaves a shiny finish with confectionery glaze if you wish.

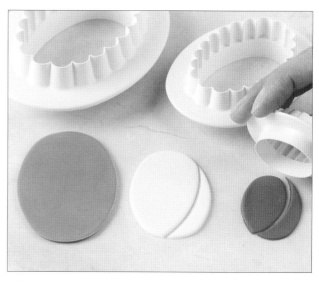

3 Also cut out some tiny red berries using the 7mm (¼in) circle cutter. Run a stitch line round the wavy edge of the swag and stick it onto the cake by first brushing the cake with water. Then attach pairs of holly leaves and a single red berry at the points.

4 Cut a large light brown oval, a medium-sized white oval and a small red oval using the three oval cutters. Cut a section off one side of the white oval and the red oval using the same cutters. Discard the small section.

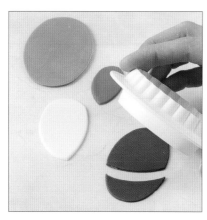

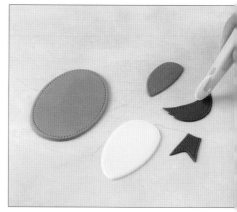

5 Cut another large oval from the mid brown paste, then turn the cutter through 90° and cut off the lower segment for the wing.

6 Remove tiny segments from the wing to create feathers. For the feet, cut two small brown squares using the 16mm (⅝in) square cutter and use the corner of the cutter to form the claws. Cut a large square using the 35mm (1½in) square cookie cutter and cut it into the tail shape using the knife and the small square cutter. Cut two legs, then cut a yellow rectangle and remove a triangle shape from one side for the beak.

7 Use the stitching wheel to mark a stitch line round the robin's breast and body pieces, tail and wing.

8 Make an eye by cutting a black circle using the 11mm (½in) circle cutter and attaching a tiny dot of white paste close to one edge. Assemble the robin on the cake, attaching the shapes by brushing the backs with water before positioning them.

9 Finally, make two long, thin sausages using red and white paste, and twist them together to make the candy-cane rope twist. It should be long enough to go all the way round the base of the cake. Place it round the cake to finish.

FALLING LEAVES

This seasonally inspired design uses freehand wheel cutting and texturing techniques to create a beautiful autumn tree. A leaf cutter and veiner add texture to the leaves. To start, edge the board with brown ribbon and secure it with non-toxic glue. Position the cake in the centre of the board.

You will need

15cm (6in) round fruit or sponge cake covered with white fondant (sugarpaste)

20.5cm (8in) round drum board covered with green fondant (sugarpaste)

Small amounts of brown modelling paste

Small amounts or red, orange, yellow, beige and rust-coloured gum paste (flower paste)

Vegetable shortening

Cornstarch (cornflour) dusting bag

Brown 15mm (⅝in) ribbon

Round cookie cutters, 85mm (3⅜in) and 65mm (2½in)

Rose leaf cutter, 11mm (½in)

Rose leaf silicone veiner

Wheel cutter

Smooth-blade kitchen knife

Artists' paintbrush

Royal icing

Piping bag and no. 2 piping nozzle

Small cranked palette knife

Non-toxic glue stick

1 Make a long, thin sausage shape using the brown modelling paste and attach it round the base of the cake. Emboss it using the wheel cutter to resemble tree bark.

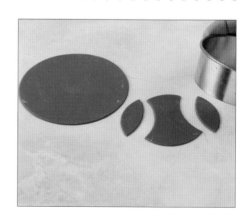

2 Cut two large brown circles using the 85mm (3⅜in) and 65mm (2½in) cookie cutters. Trim off the sides of the smaller circle using the same cutter to form the trunk.

3 Use the 85mm (3⅜in) cookie cutter to create a curve at the top of the trunk for the tree top to sit in. With the wheel cutter, cut out sections from the tree top to resemble branches.

4 Fuse the trunk to the top of the tree by rubbing both edges with water using your finger and pushing them together.

5 Cut into the branches using the wheel cutter to create finer branches, and cut a wavy line across the base of the trunk, again using the wheel cutter. Soften the join between the tree trunk and top using a paintbrush.

6 Brush off any loose sugar and add texture to the tree by marking it using the wheel cutter.

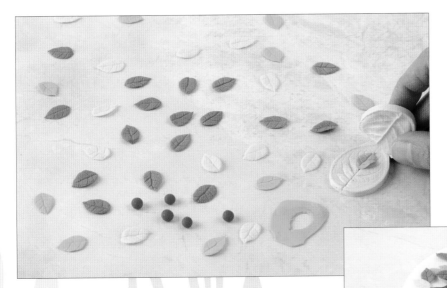

7 Using the rose leaf cutter, cut numerous leaves from orange, yellow, beige and rust-coloured gum paste. Mark on the veins using the rose leaf silicone veiner. Roll several red berries by hand.

8 Fix the tree to the top of the cake with a little water brushed on the back. Then arrange the leaves on the cake and fix by piping tiny dots of royal icing behind each of them. Finally, fix some of the leaves and berries round the base and down the side of the cake. Place the leaves at various angles, overlapping them and attaching them at the base only so they stand proud of the cake. This creates a three-dimensional effect.

Make coordinating cupcakes to go with your cake if you wish – simply decorated with leaves and berries.

51

SUMMER BUNTING

This cake is perfect for a summer tea party or a vintage-style fair. It is accompanied by matching cupcakes and displayed on an easy-to-make cake stand. The design uses modelling paste to capture the look of bunting blowing in the breeze, and edible transfers for an easy and eye-catching effect.

To display the cake, I have used two boards covered with white fondant (sugarpaste), and embossed the larger board with a pattern of small circles round the edge, marked on using an 11mm (½in) circle cutter. Both boards are edged with white ribbon, secured with non-toxic glue, then a narrower turquoise ribbon has been placed over the white ribbon on the smaller board. Begin by positioning the cake in the centre of the smaller board and edging the base with white ribbon secured with a dot of royal icing on the join.

1 Cut numerous small white circles from white modelling paste using the 11mm (½in) circle cutter. Attach them to the rim of the cake using water. To attach them in an even circle, place a round cake tin on top of the cake and work round it.

2 Cut an 8cm (3¼in) deep strip of baking parchment, long enough to fit once round the cake. Fold it into eight sections, draw a curve on the top edge and cut along the curve.

You will need

15cm (6in) round fruit or sponge cake covered with white fondant (sugarpaste)

20.5cm (8in) round drum board covered with white fondant (sugarpaste)

10cm (4in) round polystyrene cake divider

30.5cm (12in) drum board covered with white fondant (sugarpaste) for base

9 cupcakes covered with white fondant (sugarpaste), baked in pink cupcake cases

Small amounts of pink, light brown, white and red modelling paste

Edible transfers in pink, turquoise and green polka dot design

Vegetable shortening

Cornstarch (cornflour) dusting bag

Turquoise 10mm (½in) ribbon

White 15mm (⅝in) ribbon

13cm (5in) round cake tin

Circle cutters, 15mm (⅝in), 11mm (½in) and 7mm (¼in)

Square cutters, 16mm (⅝in) and 11mm (½in)

Rectangular cutter, 25 x 14mm (1 x ⅝in)

Square cookie cutters, 50mm (2in), 45mm (1¾in) and 40mm (1½in)

Round cookie cutter, 35mm (1½in)

Smooth-blade kitchen knife

Scribing tool

No. 2 piping nozzle

Baking parchment

Masking tape

Scissors

Artists' paintbrush

Royal icing

Small cranked palette knife

Non-toxic glue stick

Metal ruler

Tissue paper

3 Unfold the template round the cake with the straight edge at the base and secure the ends with a strip of masking tape. Steady the template with your hand and mark a thin line along the curved edge with the scribing tool.

4 Fix transfer sheets to rolled-out modelling paste and cut out numerous flags using the rectangular cutter. Use the corner of the cutter to cut a triangle out of one side of each rectangle to make a flag shape. Also cut out four circles using the 11mm (½in) circle cutter and four using the 15mm (⅝in) circle cutter. Cut each one in half with the knife to create the little cupcake decorations on top of the cake. Put these to one side.

5 While they are still flexible, attach the flags to the side of the cake following the scribed line. To secure each flag, brush a strip of water along the short, straight edge, then place a tiny piece of tissue under the flag to hold it away from the cake while it is drying. This will create an impression of movement. Place one of the little triangles that you cut from the flags in step 4 at the top of each swag.

6 Use each of the three square cookie cutters to cut three squares of pink modelling paste. Using one side of the cutter, cut strips with slightly curved edges.

7 Use the 16mm (⅝in) and 11mm (½in) square cutters to cut four squares (two of each size) of light brown modelling paste, then cut each one in half using a knife to make the cake bases. Mark on the lines with the knife.

8 For the cherries, roll eight tiny balls of red paste. Make the handle for the cake stand by cutting a tiny circle using the 7mm (¼in) circle cutter, and removing a pink circle from the centre using a piping nozzle. Finally, cut two thin lengths of pink modelling paste and trim them to lengths 2.5cm (1in) for the base of the cake stand and 2cm (¾in) for the handle.

9 Arrange all the elements of the cake stand on the top of the cake, using the palette knife to position them accurately. Make sure the cake stand is positioned in the centre of the cake. Paint the back of each shape with water before placing it on the cake, and reposition elements by sliding them rather than taking them off and replacing them.

10 Decorate the cupcakes using circles cut from the edible transfer sheets using the 35mm (1½in) round cookie cutter, and hand-rolled balls of red modelling paste.

11 To display the cake, place it on the cake divider placed in the centre of the larger drum board, and place the cupcakes round it.

RETRO CAKE

Funky and effective, this project gives striking results through the use of bold colours, repetition and consistent and accurate cutting. The topper's construction is inspired by disco glitter balls and papercraft techniques. To start, edge the board with red ribbon and secure it with non-toxic glue. Position the cake in the centre of the board.

You will need

15cm (6in) round fruit or sponge cake covered with white fondant (sugarpaste)

20.5cm (8in) round drum board covered with white fondant (sugarpaste)

Small amounts of red, pink and orange Mexican paste (pastillage)

White plastic cake dowel, 23cm (9in) long

Vegetable shortening

Cornstarch (cornflour) dusting bag

Red 15mm (⅝in) ribbon

Circle cutters, 30mm (1¼in), 23mm (1in) and 15mm (⅝in)

Round cookie cutters, 63mm (2½in), 50mm (2in) and 37mm (1½in)

Smooth-blade kitchen knife

Edible felt-tip pen

Set square

Artists' paintbrush

Royal icing

Piping bag and no. 2 piping nozzle

Small cranked palette knife

Non-toxic glue stick

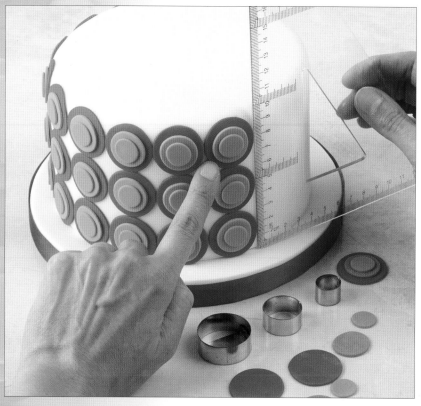

1 Cut numerous circles of red, orange and pink Mexican paste in three different sizes using the circle cutters – enough to cover the side of the the cake. Cut the largest circles from red paste, the mid-sized circles from pink paste and the smallest circles from orange paste. Create stacks of three different-sized circles, glued together with water. While the paste is still flexible, secure them to the side of the cake in regular columns of three, with the edges touching. Use the set square to ensure the columns are straight.

2 Using the round cookie cutters, cut four large circles from red paste, four medium-sized circles from orange paste and four small circles from pink paste. Cut each circle in half using a knife. Allow the half circles to dry hard overnight. Take the cake dowel, and lay three different-sized semi-circles side-by-side along its length, starting at the top with the smallest semi-circle and finishing with the largest. Mark the point on the dowel level with the base of the largest shape using the edible felt-tip pen.

3 Insert the dowel carefully into the top of the cake, up to the point marked on it in step 2. Make sure the dowel is positioned vertically in the centre of the cake.

4 Starting with the largest semi-circles, pipe dots of royal icing along the edge of one shape.

5 Stick the shape to the base of the dowel. Apply royal icing to a second red shape in the same way and attach it directly opposite the first.

6 Continue attaching the semi-circles to the dowel. Apply the next pair at right angles to the first, then place the next two pairs in between. Allow this first layer to dry thoroughly before applying the next. When you have completed all three layers, finish with a hand-rolled ball of pink paste attached to the top of the dowel.

SPACE-AGE CAKE

Ideal for any budding astronaut, this cake counts down to lift off with modelling, marbling, texturing and embellishing. A sprinkling of edible stardust lustre and sugar-ball asteroids complete the cosmic effect. To start, edge the board with black ribbon secured with non-toxic glue and position the cake in the centre.

You will need

18cm (7in) round fruit or sponge cake covered with black fondant (sugarpaste)

25.5cm (10in) round drum board covered with grey fondant (sugarpaste)

Small amounts of white, red, pale grey, yellow, lime green, black and marbled modelling paste

Small amounts of white, red, orange and yellow Mexican paste (pastillage)

Edible silver and gold lustre powder

Confectionery glaze

Edible glitter

Dipping solution

Edible silver sugar balls

Lollipop stick

Vegetable shortening

Cornstarch (cornflour) dusting bag

Black 15mm (⅝in) ribbon

Circle cutters, 30mm (1¼in), 23mm (1in), 20mm (¾in), 11mm (½in) and 7mm (¼in)

Round cookie cutters, 35mm (1½in), 30mm (1¼in) and 23mm (1in)

Square cookie cutter, 37mm (1½in)

Piping bag and no. 2 piping nozzle

Star cutter

Wheel cutter or pizza wheel

Ball tool

Smooth-blade kitchen knife

Artists' paintbrush

Royal icing

Non-toxic glue stick

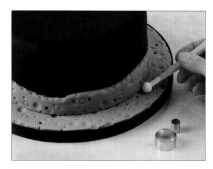

1 Use the wheel cutter to cut a band of grey modelling paste approximately 2cm (¾in) deep with one straight edge and one wavy edge, and long enough to go round the cake. Wrap it round the base of the cake and trim off the excess. Secure it using water brushed onto the cake. Emboss the cake board and the grey band using the ball tool and various circle cutters.

2 Cut the main elements of the rocket. You will need two 2.5cm (1in) deep circles of white modelling paste cut out using the 35mm (1½in) and 30mm (1¼in) cutters, and three shallow circles of red modelling paste, two 30mm (1¼in) round and one 35mm (1½in) round. Form the nose cone by hand from red modelling paste, then cut it to size using the 30mm (1¼in) circle cutter.

3 For the fins, cut two white circles of Mexican paste (pastillage) using the 35mm (1½in) round cookie cutter, then cut each one in half using a knife. With the 30mm (1¼in) circle cutter, remove a small section from each semi-circle to create the fin shape.

4 Cut a circle of grey modelling paste using the 23mm (1in) circle cutter for the base of the rocket, and a smaller grey circle using the 20mm (¾in) cutter for the port hole. Emboss the port hole using a smaller circle cutter, and mark tiny circles round the edge using a piping nozzle.

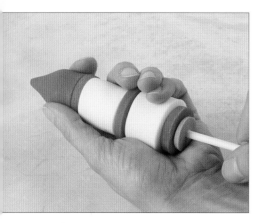

5 Stack all the elements of the rocket together in the order shown, having brushed the surface of each one with a little water to fix them together first. Push them firmly onto the lollipop stick to hold them together.

6 Mix a little edible silver lustre powder with some confectionery glaze and paint it onto the port hole. Clean your brush thoroughly with dipping solution afterwards. Attach the fins and the port hole to the rocket using small dots of royal icing applied using the piping nozzle.

7 Insert the rocket in the centre of the cake, leaving round 5cm (2in) of the lollipop stick showing.

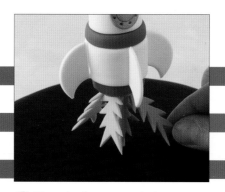

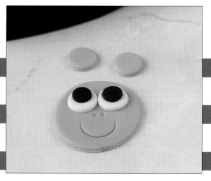

8 Cut six or seven squares using the 37mm (1½in) cookie cutter from red, orange and yellow Mexican paste. Cut the squares in half to form rectangles. Cut out triangular segments from each side using a knife to create flames.

9 Allow the flames to dry hard then attach them round the base of the rocket, sticking them in place with a small dot of royal icing applied to the end of each flame.

10 The alien's head is made from a 30mm (1¼in) circle cut from green modelling paste. Cut the antennae and white eye parts using an 11mm (½in) circle cutter, and the black eye parts using a 7mm (¼in) cutter. Attach the white and black eye parts to the face, and mark on the mouth with a circle cutter. Use the piping nozzle to mark on the nostrils.

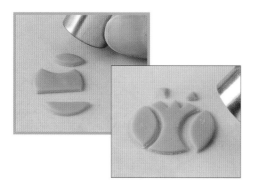

11 To make the alien's body, cut a circle using the 23mm (1in) circle cutter, cut off the base with a knife, then create a neck using a smaller circle cutter. For the arms, use the 23mm (1in) circle cutter to cut out a circle, and use the same cutter to create the sides. Cut out the fingers using the knife.

12 Cut two green sticks for the antennae, then put all the elements together on the side of the cake. Secure them using water brushed onto the back of each shape. Add a tiny dot of royal icing to the eyes using the piping nozzle to really bring them to life.

13 Cut a variety of circles and star shapes from modelling paste in various colours to make the stars and planets. Use marbled modelling paste to create a planet effect. Attach them randomly to the cake.

14 Sprinkle edible glitter over the top of the cake, and add a few silver sugar balls to complete this out-of-this-world cake.

FAIRYTALE CASTLE

You don't need a magic wand to make this fairytale castle cake, just a wheel cutter and some square and flower-shaped cutters. Pretty pastels and pinks will delight the guests at any princess party, while matching mini crown cakes make lovely gifts for them to take home. To start, edge the board with pink ribbon secured with non-toxic glue and position the cake in the centre. Edge the base of the cake with white ribbon, and the base of each mini cake with pink ribbon. Secure these ribbons with a small dot of royal icing placed on the join.

You will need

25.5cm (10in) round fruit or sponge cake covered with pale pink fondant (sugarpaste)

30.5cm (12in) round drum board covered with white fondant (sugarpaste)

5cm (2in) mini cakes covered with white fondant (sugarpaste)

Small amounts of pastel orange, yellow, green, blue, lilac, dove grey, white, pale pink, mid pink and dark pink modelling paste

Ivory sugar pearls

Paper template for landscape scene (page 76)

Vegetable shortening

Cornstarch (cornflour) dusting bag

Pink 15mm (⅝in) ribbon

White 15mm (⅝in) ribbon

23cm (9in) round cake board or tin to cut round

30.5cm (12in) round drum board

15cm (6in) round cake tin to shape rainbow

Small heart plunger cutters in two different sizes

Square cookie cutters, 54mm (2¼in) and 25mm (1in)

Blossom plunger cutters, 9mm (⅜in) and 7mm (¼in)

Parallel wheel cutter or knife

Smooth-blade kitchen knife

Royal icing

No. 2 piping nozzle

Ball tool

Artists' paintbrush

Small cranked palette knife

Non-toxic glue stick

Metal ruler

1 Make the rainbow on a separate 30.5cm (12in) drum board using modelling paste, following the instructions on page 24. Shape it round a 23cm (9in) cake tin. Leave it to dry until firm, then slide it across to the top of the cake using a palette knife. Position the rainbow towards the top of the cake and gently slip a moistened paintbrush under the edges of the rainbow to fix it in place.

2 Cut the grass section from green paste, using the template supplied on page 76. Position the grass on the cake, first brushing the cake underneath with water.

3 Make the components of the castle. Cut two squares from lilac paste using the 54mm (2¼in) cookie cutter. Cut one square in half to make two rectangles and mark two lines across the top of each one using either the knife or a parallel wheel cutter. For the turrets, cut a square of mid pink paste, cut it into two rectangles and cut off the sides to make triangles.

4 Use the knife to mark a brick pattern on the remaining square and cut out the crenellations using the tip of a heart plunger cutter.

5 For the door, cut a mid pink rectangle 30 x 20mm (1¼ x ¾in) with a knife, draw a line down the centre, and mark on the door knobs using the end of a piping nozzle. Cut out the path by hand from dove-grey modelling paste using a knife, and trim off the top and bottom. Rub gently to create a curve. Emboss the surface using a ball tool.

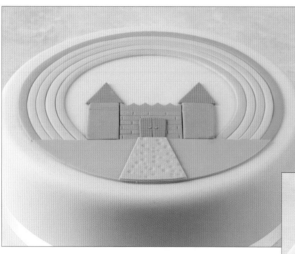

Tip
Remember that if you need to reposition a shape, don't try to remove it – simply slide it into its new position.

6 Assemble the castle on the top of the cake, first brushing the cake with water to hold the pieces in place.

7 Cut out the pale pink hearts using the heart plunger cutters and make little blue flags from small rectangles with triangular sections cut from one side. The tops of the flag poles are flattened balls of dark pink paste. Fix these elements in place with a little water, using a paintbrush to manoeuvre them into position.

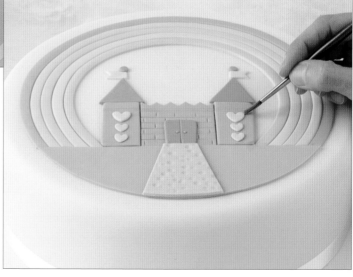

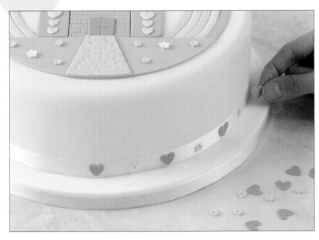

8 Use the blossom plunger cutters to make approximately eight small white and pale pink flowers, and attach them to the grass with dots of royal icing. Cut more pale pink flowers and some dark pink hearts, and attach them in an alternating pattern to the ribbon, again with dots of royal icing.

9 For the crowns on the mini cakes, cut 1cm (½in) deep strips of pale pink modelling paste and cut out heart shapes along their lengths using the smaller of the two heart plunger cutters. Use the tip of the cutter to create the points along the top edge of each strip. Curl each strip round to form a crown and brush the join with water to seal. Attach an ivory sugar pearl to each point using a dot of royal icing.

ART DECO

This stylish cake shows how you can use a template and cutters to create sugar transfers that enable accurate and repeatable decorative patterns to be applied over any smooth cake covering. To start, edge the board with black ribbon secured with non-toxic glue and position the larger cake in the centre. Edge the base of the cake with black ribbon and secure it with a small dot of royal icing placed on the join.

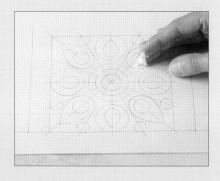

1 Make a copy of the template on a sheet of printer paper and slide it into a plastic document wallet (see instructions on pages 78–79). Use your fingers to spread an even layer of vegetable shortening over the plastic document wallet to complete the transfer backing.

2 Roll out the modelling paste between spacers to ensure an even thickness. Cut out all of the outer shapes, using the picture for guidance. As you cut each shape out, place it on the corresponding part of the template to create the transfer. Cut out the inner shapes after you've placed the outer shapes on the template, otherwise they may distort when you pick them up. Don't place the layered elements on the template – these will be added once the design has been transferred to the cake.

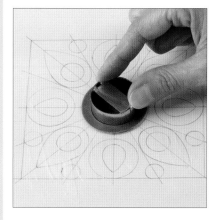

Note
If your cake is a slightly different size from that shown, or you are using different-sized cutters, the templates provided may not work. If this is the case, you can create your own version of the template relatively easily by following the instructions provided on page 79.

3 When all the elements are in place, paint each one with water. Avoid wetting the transfer backing.

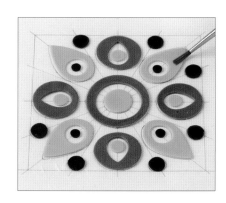

You will need

10cm (4in) and 15cm (6in) sponge or fruit cube cakes covered with white fondant (sugarpaste)

25.5cm (10in) square drum board covered with black fondant (sugarpaste)

Cake dowels to support the top tier

Small amounts of black, lime green and purple modelling paste

Edible silver sugar balls

White vegetable shortening

Cornstarch (cornflour) dusting bag

Black 15mm (⅝in) ribbon

Circle cutters, 45mm (1¾in), 30mm (1¼in), 20mm (¾in), 15mm (⅝in), 10mm (½in) and 7mm (¼in)

Petal cutters, lengths 40mm (1½in) and 20mm (¾in)

Templates (pages 77–78)

2 plastic document wallets

Artists' paintbrush

Royal icing

Non-toxic glue stick

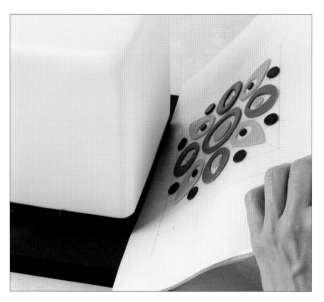

4 Carefully pick up the transfer and align the base and side guides of the transfer with the bottom and sides of the cake.

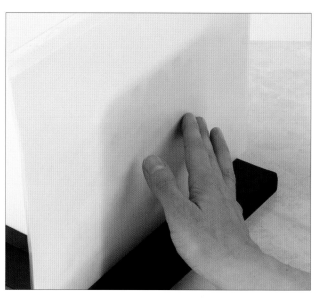

5 Press the transfer onto the surface of the cake, rubbing all over the back of it with your fingers to make sure the shapes adhere firmly.

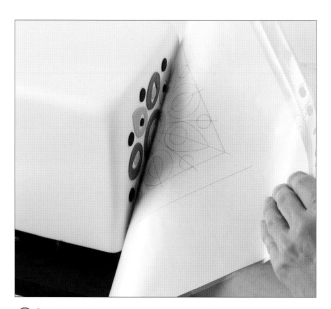

6 Gently peel back the transfer backing, leaving the shapes attached to the cake.

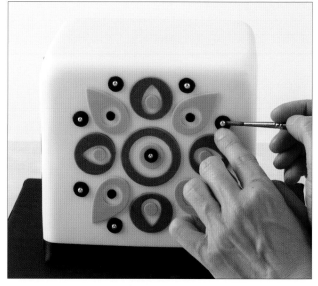

7 Allow the shapes to dry for an hour or two; during this time attach the design to the remaining three sides. When completely dry, rub off the shortening with an artists' paintbrush and neaten any untidy edges. Attach the remaining small black circle in the middle of the central shape with a little water, and attach the silver sugar balls using small dots of royal icing.

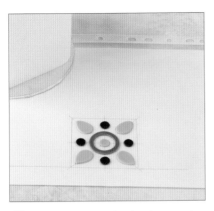

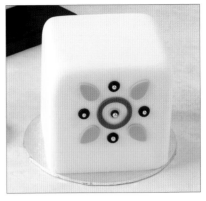

8 Create the transfer for the top tier of the cake, cut out the shapes and place them on the transfer in the same way.

9 Transfer the design to the side of the smaller cake.

10 Attach the silver sugar balls using dots of royal icing and decorate the other three sides of the cake in the same way.

11 Dowel the bottom tier and secure the smaller cake on top of the larger one centrally with royal icing. Edge the base of the top tier with black ribbon.

WEDDING CAKE

This romantic wedding cake has been given a contemporary twist with its single deep tier. The stylised sugar flowers make an eye-catching statement and the colours can be adapted to match any wedding theme. Decorative borders and sugar buttons add style, and sugar pearls and lustre effects complete the look. Begin by edging the board with peach ribbon, securing it using non-toxic glue, then stack the cake using cake dowels.

You will need

10cm (4in), 20.5cm (8in) and 25.5cm (10in) round fruit or sponge cakes, each 7.5cm (3in) deep, placed on same-size hard boards and covered with ivory fondant (sugarpaste)

15cm (6in) round fruit or sponge cake, 15cm (6in) deep, placed on same-size hard board and covered with ivory fondant (sugarpaste)

30.5cm (12in) round drum board covered with ivory fondant (sugarpaste)

Cake dowels to support tiers

Small amounts of gum paste (flower paste) in three different shades of peach

Pearl lustre powder

Dipping solution

Edible sugar pearls

Vegetable shortening

Cornstarch (cornflour) dusting bag

Peach 15mm (⅝in) ribbon

Circle cutters, 30mm (1¼in), 25mm (1in), 15mm (⅝in), 10mm (½in) and 8mm (¼in)

Large petal cutters in various sizes

Piping bag and nos 1 and 2 piping nozzles

Ball tool

Set square

Foam mat

Kitchen paper

Stitching wheel

Parallel wheel cutter

Smooth-blade kitchen knife

Artists' paintbrush

Royal icing

Non-toxic glue stick

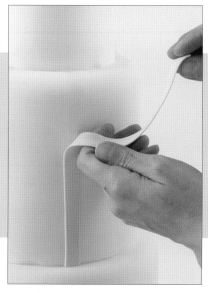

1 Using a parallel wheel cutter, cut two 8mm (¼in) strips of pale peach paste, each long enough to extend up the side of the 15cm (6in) deep tier and across the top to the base of the top tier. Run a stitch line along each side of each strip using the stitching wheel. Attach a strip to the front and back of the 15cm (6in) tier by first coating the cake underneath with water.

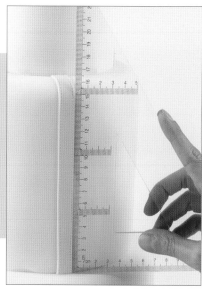

2 Use a set square to make sure the strip is straight, and adjust it if necessary by sliding it over the surface of the cake (not by removing it).

Tip

Ensure you use sufficient cake dowels to support each tier.

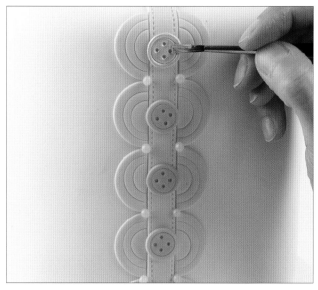

3 Cut numerous circles from pale peach paste using a 30mm (1¼in) circle cutter. Cut each one in half and emboss each semi-circle using two smaller cutters. Paint water onto the cake on either side of the two strips and attach the semi-circles as shown. Put the remaining semi-circles to one side.

4 Attach sugar pearls to the points where the shapes touch using dots of royal icing. Make twelve buttons using a 10mm (½in) circle cutter and emboss them with a slightly smaller cutter. Make the four tiny holes using the end of a no. 2 piping nozzle. Attach the buttons to the cake as shown above. Keep two buttons back for finishing the statement flowers. Paint all the flowers with pearl lustre powder mixed with a little dipping solution.

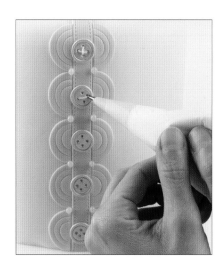

5 Use the no. 1 piping nozzle to add two thin threads of white royal icing across each button.

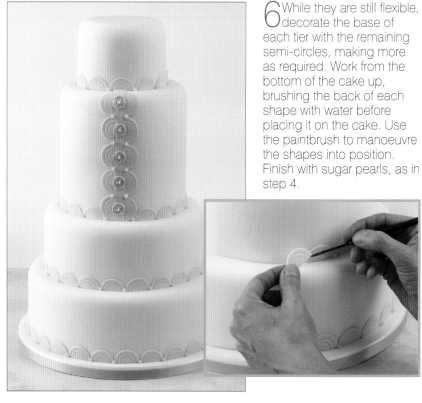

6 While they are still flexible, decorate the base of each tier with the remaining semi-circles, making more as required. Work from the bottom of the cake up, brushing the back of each shape with water before placing it on the cake. Use the paintbrush to manoeuvre the shapes into position. Finish with sugar pearls, as in step 4.

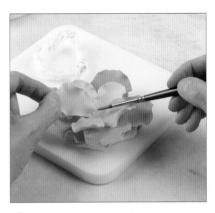

7 For each of the accent flowers, cut five petals from dark peach-coloured paste using the largest petal cutter. Working on a foam mat, create folds in the edges of the petals using the ball tool (see page 25).

8 Take a piece of kitchen paper, twist it into a tight sausage shape and curl it round to form a ring. Place your five petals evenly in the ring to form a flower shape. Stick the centres of the petals together using water and press down firmly in the centre of the flower to cup the petals before they dry.

9 Repeat steps 7 and 8 using a slightly smaller petal cutter and peach-coloured paste in a shade lighter. Secure these petals in the middle of the first set.

10 Repeat using a smaller petal cutter and the palest peach-coloured paste, and secure these in the flower centre. Finish with one of the buttons you made earlier.

11 Attach the two large flowers to the cake using large dots of royal icing applied to the backs.

TEMPLATES

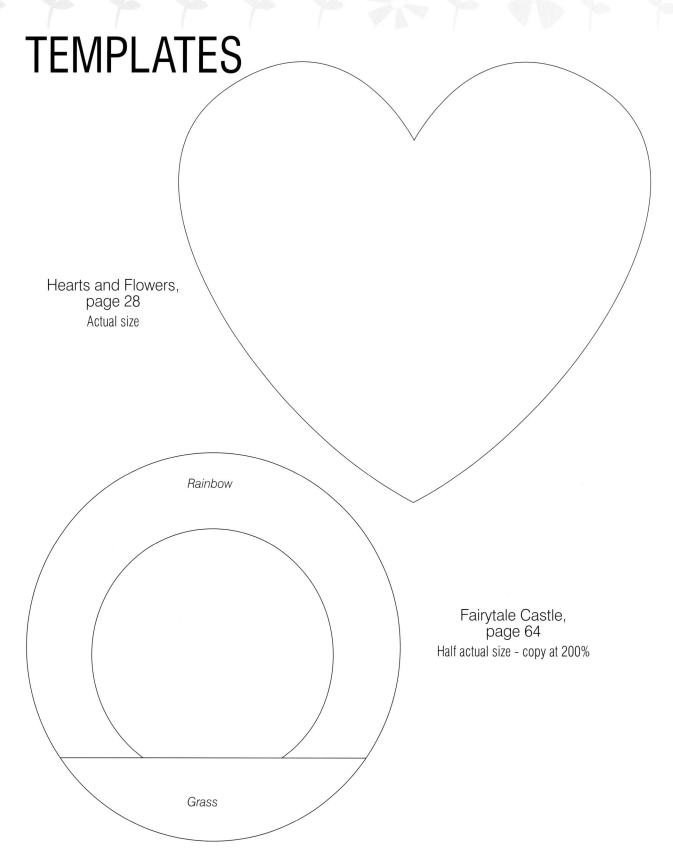

Hearts and Flowers,
page 28
Actual size

Rainbow

Grass

Fairytale Castle,
page 64
Half actual size - copy at 200%

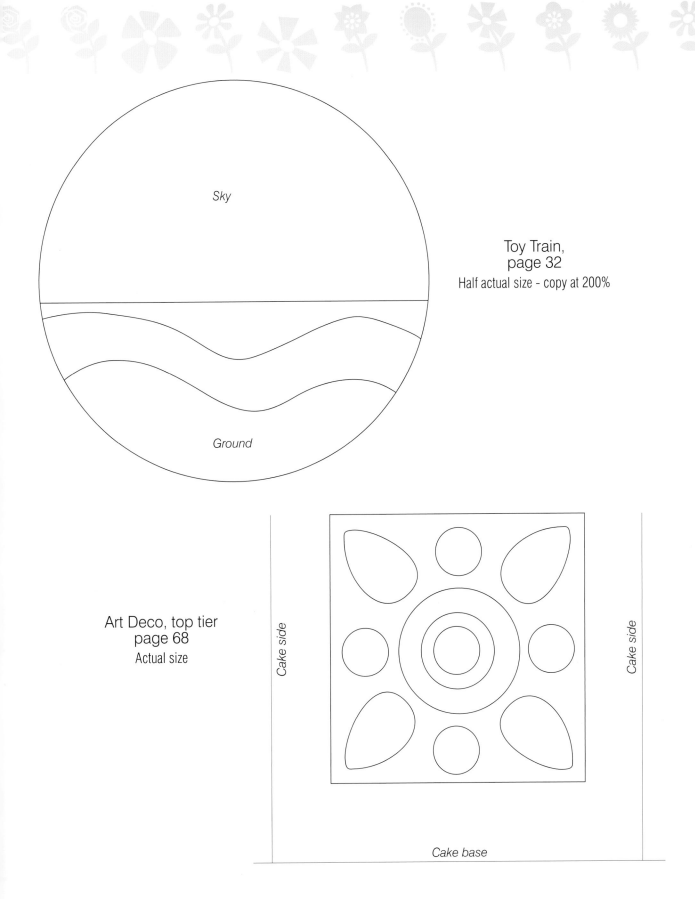

Sky

Ground

Toy Train,
page 32
Half actual size - copy at 200%

Art Deco, top tier
page 68
Actual size

Cake side

Cake side

Cake base

Art Deco, base tier
page 68
Actual size

Cake side

Cake side

Cake base

Creating your own pattern and template

If your cake is a different size from that shown on page 68, or you are using different-sized cutters, the templates provided opposite may not work. Instead, you can make your own version of the templates by simply following the steps below.

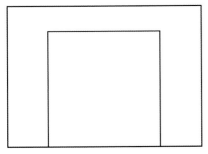

1 Measure the width and height of one of the sides of the iced cake. Draw an equivalent shape in the middle of a sheet of A4 paper, with the bottom edge of the paper forming the bottom edge of the shape. The two vertical lines will help with the sideways alignment when applying the transfer.

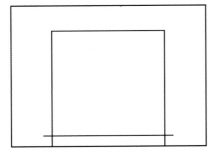

2 Measure the width of your ribbon trim and draw a parallel line at an equivalent distance from the bottom edge of the paper.

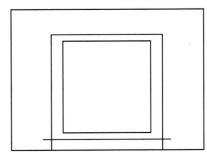

3 Mark the area to be covered by your template on the paper. In this case it is a square.

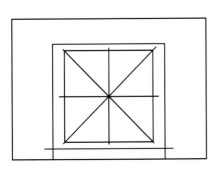

4 Divide the area into eight equal sections.

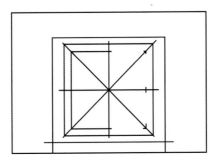

5 Mark the position guides for the shapes that will make up the pattern. You can do this by drawing a second square using the diagonal section lines to guide its position. Then rub out the parts of the square between the section lines leaving just the position guides.

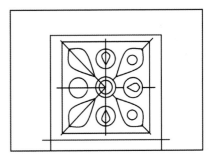

6 Develop your template pattern by positioning your cutters according to the section lines and position guides and drawing round them.

INDEX